JACK THORNE

Jack Thorne's plays for the stage include *Harry Potter and the Cursed Child* (Palace Theatre, London, since 2016, and Lyric Theatre, New York, since 2018; winner of the 2017 Olivier Award for Best New Play and the 2018 Tony Award for Best Play); a reimagining of *A Christmas Carol* by Charles Dickens (Old Vic Theatre, 2017, 2018, 2019); *the end of history...* (Royal Court Theatre, 2019); a musical adaptation of *King Kong* (Broadway Theatre, New York, 2018); a new version of Georg Büchner's *Woyzeck* (Old Vic Theatre, 2017); *Junkyard* (Headlong/Bristol Old Vic/Rose Theatre Kingston/Theatr Clwyd, 2017); *The Solid Life of Sugar Water* (Graeae Theatre Company); *Hope* (Royal Court Theatre, London, 2014); adaptations of *Let the Right One In* (National Theatre of Scotland at Dundee Rep, the Royal Court and the Apollo Theatre, London, 2013/14) and *Stuart: A Life Backwards* (Underbelly, Edinburgh, and tour, 2013); *Mydidae* (Soho, 2012; Trafalgar Studios, 2013); an adaptation of Friedrich Dürrenmatt's *The Physicists* (Donmar Warehouse, 2012); *Bunny* (Underbelly, Edinburgh, 2010; Soho, 2011); *2nd May 1997* (Bush, 2009); *Burying Your Brother in the Pavement* (National Theatre Connections, 2008); *When You Cure Me* (Bush, 2005; Radio 3's Drama on Three, 2006); *Fanny and Faggot* (Pleasance, Edinburgh, 2004 and 2007; Finborough, 2007; English Theatre of Bruges, 2007; Trafalgar Studios, 2007); and *Stacy* (Tron, 2006; Arcola, 2007; Trafalgar Studios, 2007).

His radio plays include *Left at the Angel* (Radio 4, 2007), an adaptation of *The Hunchback of Notre Dame* (2009), and an original play *People Snogging in Public Places* (Radio 3's Wire slot, 2009).

For television, Jack has five BAFTAs for his work on *National Treasure* (Best Mini-Series, 2017); *This is England '90* (Best Mini-Series, 2016); *Don't Take My Baby* (Best Single Drama, 2016); *The Fades* (Best Drama Series, 2012); *This is England '88* (Best Mini-Series, 2012). His other writing for television includes the BBC adaptation of Philip Pullman's *His Dark Materials*, *CripTales*, *The Eddy*, *The Accident*, *The Virtues*, *Kiri*, *Electric Dreams*, *The Last Panthers*, *Glue*, *Shameless*, *Skins* and *Cast-Offs*.

His work for film includes the features *Enola Holmes*, *The Secret Garden*, *Radioactive*, *Dirt Music*, *Wonder*, *War Book*, *A Long Way Down* and *The Scouting Book for Boys*.

Jack is a patron of Graeae Theatre Company, an associate artist of The Old Vic, and a fellow of the Royal Society of Literature.

AFTER LIFE

Written by Jack Thorne

Adapted from the film by Hirokazu Kore-eda

Concept by Bunny Christie, Jeremy Herrin and Jack Thorne

NICK HERN BOOKS

London

www.nickhernbooks.co.uk

A Nick Hern Book

After Life first published in Great Britain in 2021 as a paperback original by Nick Hern Books Limited, The Glasshouse, 49a Goldhawk Road, London W12 8QP

After Life copyright © 2021 Jack Thorne and Disney Enterprises, Inc.

Jack Thorne has asserted his moral right to be identified as the author of this adaptation

Cover image: Photography by Simon Pais; Art direction and design by National Theatre Graphic Design Studio

Designed and typeset by Nick Hern Books, London
Printed in the UK by Mimeo Ltd, Huntingdon, Cambridgeshire PE29 6XX

A CIP catalogue record for this book is available from the British Library

ISBN 978 1 83904 014 6

After Life was first performed as a National Theatre/Headlong
co-production in the Dorfman auditorium of the National Theatre,
London, on 9 June 2021 (previews from 2 June). The cast was as
follows:

GUIDES
ONE	Danielle Henry
TWO	Luke Thallon
THREE	Simon Startin
FOUR	Millicent Wong
FIVE	Kevin McMonagle

GUIDED
OBAFEMI TAYLOR	Olatunji Ayofe
YOUNG HIROKAZU MOCHIZUKI /	
HENRY THOMPSON	Nino Furuhata
JILL SMART /	
YOUNG BEATRICE	Maddie Holliday
HIROKAZU MOCHIZUKI	Togo Igawa
KATIE MOCHIZUKI	Anoushka Lucas
ACTOR HAROLD /	
GRAHAM JENKINS	Jack James Ryan
BEATRICE KILLICK	June Watson

Director	Jeremy Herrin
Set and Costume Designer	Bunny Christie
Lighting Designer	Neil Austin
Sound Designer	Tom Gibbons
Movement Director	Shelley Maxwell
Music	Orlando Weeks
Music Production and	
Additional Composition	Sam Hudson Scott
Video Designer	Max Spielbichler
Company Voice Work	Jeannette Nelson
Staff Director	TD. Moyo
Literal Translator	Jo Allen

Commissioned and developed by the National Theatre's New Work
Department.

By special arrangement with Buena Vista Theatrical.

For my beautiful friend
Fred Hodder
1980–2001

'Within the bowels of these elements,
Where we are tortured and remain forever.
Hell hath no limits, nor is circumscribed
In one self place, for where we are is hell,
And where hell is, there must we ever be.
And, to conclude, when all the world dissolves,
And every creature shall be purified,
All places shall be hell that is not heaven.'

Doctor Faustus, *Christopher Marlowe*

Characters

GUIDES
ONE, *female, thirties*
TWO, *male, mid- to late twenties*
THREE, *male, early forties*
FOUR, *female, seventeen*
FIVE, *male, fifties*

GUIDED
BEATRICE KILLICK, *female, ninety-one*
HIROKAZU MOCHIZUKI, *male, seventy-four*
OBAFEMI TAYLOR, *male, twenty-one*
JILL SMART, *female, thirteen*
HENRY THOMPSON, *male, thirties*
ACTOR HAROLD, *young male*
ACTRESS BEATRICE, *young female*
ACTOR HIROKAZU, *male, thirties*
KATIE MOCHIZUKI, *female, thirties*

ACT ONE

Scene One

The audience enter a big and impersonal room.

There is something magnificent about it, there's something hugely bureaucratic about it.

But most importantly of all –

– there is a stench of death about the place.

Two people, TWO *and* FOUR, *are cleaning away the debris and shoes. The debris is strange. The shoes are stranger.*

TWO *picks up the shoes and puts them in a box. Which he then seals and marks with yesterday's date. Whilst* FOUR *sweeps the rest away.*

After he's packed the shoes and she's swept the floor, they get out mops, and carefully and swiftly mop the floor. They're good cleaners.

All trace of what was is removed.

TWO. Do we have clearance?

He gets a nod from stage management.

They leave the stage.

And then a bell tolls. Three times.

Our guides appear carrying chairs.

Suddenly the lights change.

And steam comes in from all the entrances as they are sealed.

ONE, TWO, THREE, FOUR *and* FIVE *enter the space.*

FIVE *looks around the gathered.*

FIVE. You'd hope we were better looking. With an entrance like that, right?

'MONDAY' appears projected onto the haze.

Good morning. Good afternoon. Good evening. I think you understand the situation but I am obliged to inform you officially. Yesterday you passed away. I am very sorry for your loss.

He smiles.

You will be staying here with us for one week. Everyone has a private room – and you will be fed, watered and well looked after. No spa facilities I regret to say, as one woman – an American – asked the other week. She wanted to – steam. But we encourage you to relax and make yourself comfortable. However, while you're here, there is one thing we must ask you to do.

He looks around.

We would like you to choose one memory, which is most meaningful or precious to you. One which creates a feeling you'll be happy to – endure within. There is a time limit for this of three days. Once you've chosen your memory our staff will do their best to recreate it. On Saturday they will be presented to you and you will move on, taking only that memory with you.

He looks around the faces.

This process can be difficult, it can be painful even, but we are dedicated to try and make it as beautiful as possible for you. Or as beautiful as we can without steam. Thank you for listening. May your memories make you fly.

Scene Two

FOUR *is pacing up and down.* TWO *sits behind a desk.*
Reading a book.

FOUR. What are you reading this week?

   TWO *raises up his book.*

   A new one. Again. How do you do it?

TWO. Perseverance.

   There's a moment between them. FOUR *starts pacing again.*

FOUR. I always get so fucking nervous before these things.

TWO. Do you have to use that word?

FOUR. I'm sorry. I get so – mega-nervous.

TWO. 'Mega.'

   A buzzer sounds.

FIVE. Number 286.

FOUR. There isn't enough of us. Even Five says so.

   TWO *puts down his book. He looks at the time.*

TWO. Are you ready?

FOUR. I'm ready.

TWO. Go on then.

FOUR. Number 286.

BEATRICE. Here.

   She stands.

TWO. Good morning.

   BEATRICE *looks dazed.*

   Help her. Help her.

FOUR *runs up to help her.*

Are you comfortable with the step?

BEATRICE *comes down the step.*

BEATRICE (*quietly*). I'm fine, dear.

FOUR. You are Mrs Beatrice Killick?

BEATRICE (*quietly*). Miss.

As they reach TWO, TWO *indicates on the form where* FOUR *has got it wrong.*

FOUR. Miss. I'm sorry. I need your date of birth – for confirmation.

TWO *pulls out a chair for* BEATRICE *to sit.*

BEATRICE (*still very quietly*). I was born on 3rd April, 1930.

There's a silence.

TWO. Miss Killick, we are – needless to say – very sorry for your loss.

BEATRICE. Yes. He said. I have a cat.

TWO. Is this the memory you're thinking about?

BEATRICE. No. I have a cat. At home. A cat. I'm scared for it.

TWO. Of course you are.

BEATRICE. Can you help?

TWO. Sadly not.

BEATRICE. No one will feed it.

TWO. They will.

BEATRICE. No one will find it.

TWO. Is it hidden?

BEATRICE. Only in my house. But no one will find me.

There's another silence.

TWO. I can't help you with that matter. But maybe we can talk about your memory?

BEATRICE. I don't care about the memory. I care about my cat.

A buzzer sounds. The lights switch off on this side and light up on the other side of the room where ONE *stands waiting for her client.*

ONE. Number 748.

OBAFEMI TAYLOR *stands.*

OBAFEMI. Me.

He walks down to her.

You don't look like an angel.

ONE. Charming of you to say so.

OBAFEMI. But you're a sort of angel, right?

ONE. I wouldn't say so, no. That's not the way, we actually have stairs for a reason...

OBAFEMI. Does everyone end up here?

ONE. Yes.

OBAFEMI. Everyone?

ONE. Yes.

OBAFEMI. Regardless of good or bad?

ONE. You're referring to the idea of heaven and hell?

OBAFEMI. The 'idea'?

ONE (*wincing*). That was perhaps crudely put.

OBAFEMI. You're really telling me this is all there is? Okay. That's bullshit. Okay.

A buzzer sounds.

FIVE. Number 114.

We cut again. JILL SMART *is desperate to please.*

JILL. It was a little far away but we decided to go on that ride… the one called the Tower of Terror.

TWO. The Tower of Terror? Okay.

JILL. It was – we'd just had pancakes – the queue took forever, but once we were on it. I sat by Noma, my friend, and we held hands all the way around, screaming our heads off. And laughing. It was – could I have that?

TWO. You want to be terrified – for eternity?

JILL. I want to be happy. That was happy. Is that me done?

A buzzer sounds.

FIVE. Number 677.

We cut to THREE *facing a silent man,* HENRY THOMPSON.

THREE. Perfectly right, save your voice, I would.

HENRY *still says nothing.*

Personally, I enjoy the quiet.

There's still nothing.

As my father always said, speak only when you've got something to say.

HENRY *screams loudly.*

A final buzzer sounds.

FIVE. Number 971.

We switch back a final time. To TWO *facing a rather staid-looking man –* HIROKAZU MOCHIZUKI.

HIROKAZU. Do you mean something fun or something that made me happy?

TWO. A memory that is most precious or meaningful to you.

HIROKAZU *looks up at him.*

HIROKAZU. Most precious or meaningful, yes.

He thinks.

TWO. You don't have to come up with the favourite straight away – we can talk through a few.

HIROKAZU. It's harder than it seems, isn't it? Such a large decision.

TWO. For instance, we could talk about some hobbies you enjoyed.

HIROKAZU. They always felt such a waste of time.

TWO. What did you enjoy about your work?

HIROKAZU. I did some hobbies – bridge, chess, fishing occasionally – and Katie made me start cycling –

TWO. Katie was your wife –

HIROKAZU. Forty-three years. She's not here – I did rather wonder – people do say there is a possibility of reuniting –

TWO. Only in memory.

HIROKAZU. Understood. Sorry.

TWO. Perhaps we could talk about your wedding day?

HIROKAZU. Very stressful. My mother drank – too much.

TWO. Perhaps a particular moment of – intimacy –

HIROKAZU *blushes.*

I'm not referring to – I'm referring to –

HIROKAZU. I understood.

There's a silence. He's really struggling.

TWO. Did you take holidays?

HIROKAZU. Regularly. Once I even took her on a surprise holiday –

TWO. That sounds promising –

HIROKAZU. It didn't have the impact I hoped.

He sits back.

There must be so many – how did you put it?

TWO. Most precious or meaningful.

HIROKAZU *looks up, his face one of pure pain.*

HIROKAZU. I will think of something good.

Scene Three

ONE *moves forward and looks up at the sky. She frowns.*

TWO *moves past her.*

She nods.

TWO. What?

ONE. You're in a worst state than me.

TWO. Mondays. I hate Mondays.

FOUR *hurries to catch* TWO *up.*

FOUR. The notes from today –

TWO. Oh, yes.

FOUR. I think they're possibly the dullest notes I've ever typed, possibly the dullest notes anyone has ever typed. We cannot help your cat.

ONE. Cat worry. Never a good one.

TWO. Worried no one will find her – and so no one will find her cat.

FOUR. I mean, you feel like saying – if no one finds your body – the cat has got meat to eat.

ONE. Ouch.

TWO. Thank you.

FOUR. What?

>FOUR *looks at him, she knows she's being dismissed, she moves on tenderly.*

ONE. She's learning.

TWO. Monday is a map, isn't it? A map of what the week will be. That's why we hate it.

ONE. My map's got a coffee stain on it.

TWO. I always think – what if this is the week – what if this is the week where I fail everyone –

ONE. If my husband was here now, he'd say, 'Failure is just a word.'

>*She looks for something from* TWO, *he gives her nothing.*

>But to be honest, he was an arsehole – and a failure. You never have – failed everyone –

TWO. Just some.

>ONE *looks at him.*

ONE. Are you okay?

TWO. This Monday feels different. Worse – or just – different.

ONE. Maybe good will come, Mr Different.

TWO. I hope you're right – sorry – sorry – very indulgent – thinking.

ONE. Not to worry. We'll talk about me next time.

>TWO *looks at her and laughs.*

TWO. We will.

>*They hesitate a moment more.*

>Well, plenty to do.

Scene Four

ONE, TWO, THREE, FOUR *and* FIVE *are looking up at the projector.*

FIVE. Next.

> HIROKAZU *appears behind our actors, but they keep looking up as if he's ahead.*

TWO. Hirokazu Mochizuki.

> *The guides have files with letters on the front spelling out 'TUESDAY' when they stand in perfect configuration.*

> Haven't got to the bottom of him. We talk things through and he says – no, not that, it's not good enough –

THREE. A digger.

TWO. He's just searching for a – I don't know – a legacy.

FIVE. Maybe remind him that legacy is a problem for the living.

TWO. I've requested tapes. I'm taking a private look.

FIVE. Good. Next.

> OBAFEMI *flashes up.*

ONE. Obafemi Taylor. He's trouble. He doesn't want to choose anything, and he keeps taking me down cul-de-sacs and then dumping me on the other side.

THREE. Like what?

ONE. Well, first he asked whether his moment could be catching a Malteser perfectly in his mouth. Next he asked: Can I pick a dream?

FOUR. Can they pick a dream?

FIVE. What did you say?

ONE. I asked him to describe a dream. He described one about being on a multicoloured beach and –

OBAFEMI *appears again behind them.*

OBAFEMI. I'm running – fast – faster than feels real to me – faster than I remember being able to run –

ONE. Why are you running fast?

OBAFEMI. Because I'm being followed by this hyper-energetic guy.

ONE. The man gains on him and gains on him until he – the dreamer – starts to float away from him.

OBAFEMI. Float up. Float so far up. Float almost into space. And this guy – this hyper-energetic guy – is just stuck there on the sand – and I am laughing – laughing so hard at him.

ONE. He asked if we could recreate the relief of floating.

FIVE. And you said...

ONE. I said why do you think that dream is important to you?

FIVE. Fantastic.

ONE. And he said –

OBAFEMI. It *isn't* important to me – I'm just exploring the possibilities.

THREE. I'll take him. Reassign him to me.

ONE. No. No. I'll crack him.

FIVE. Of course you will. Next.

And then BEATRICE *is visible in a different place entirely.*

TWO. Beatrice Killick.

FIVE. You like her.

FOUR. She was very worried about her cat...

TWO. First meeting, awful, second meeting – we had a bit of a breakthrough.

FOUR. It was magic. She was humming a tune as she came in and he asked her what it was...

BEATRICE. I wasn't humming anything…

TWO *talks up to* BEATRICE.

TWO. It sounded similar to 'Don't Sit Under the Apple Tree'?

There's a hesitation. She brightens.

BEATRICE. Oh. It might have been. We did – he was one of our favourites… when we went dancing. The Andrews Sisters, Glenn Miller, Perry Como, 'The Sparrow Dance' or 'The Red Shoes'.

TWO. Where did you dance?

BEATRICE. Fairbrass Hall. On Milman Street. Or sometimes we'd go to the Cooksiedaisy – that was just by the bus depot – on United Lane or was it – well, doesn't matter. Fairbrass was where the best dancing was.

TWO. And you always wanted to be where the best dancing was…

BEATRICE. Have I told you about my cat?

TWO. You have.

BEATRICE. I, uh, I shouldn't have left it. I should have found it a home. I always said I couldn't love anything else, I wanted to be the one who died next, the cat came to me by mistake –

TWO. Beatrice, I'm interested in Fairbrass Hall. What else can you tell me about then – can you sing me any of those songs?

She looks at him, she shuts her eyes, she's trying hard.

BEATRICE. I used to remember everything, you know. Even went on some quizzes on the television. *Fifteen to One*, I went on *Fifteen to One* twice. But now – it all just – passes so quickly… (*Sings.*) 'A little girl wearing shoes of red…'

She thinks. She sings on.

'Destined to dance until she is wed.'

She looks up.

And then you'd link arms with your partner – wave your handkerchief and everyone in the room would sing 'She took them off and away she fled.' There was fun to it.

TWO. Who was with you? Who did you partner with?

BEATRICE. Anyway, the James family – who ran the butcher's – always had ideas above their station – and one night – both of the daughters – wore these red dresses. And my older brother – Harold – he thought these red dresses were something special, you see, and he went all over Bolton to find the right exact material and then I knocked it up on the sewing machine.

TWO *smiles and nods*.

We went with it to the Fairbrass. And the lighting was quite the thing there. And I caught my brother's eye as I was – dancing with – Ted Frampton – son of the publican, who always smelt of soap – Harold was at the back, they were serving sugar bread, daffodil cake and tea.

FOUR. Sugar bread?

BEATRICE. White slices with sugar sprinkled on. Dripping too if you had an extra ha'penny. Harold smiled at me and I knew – I looked exactly right. I don't know if you've ever looked exactly right for someone but it was – it was nice… And he put a whole half-piece of sugar bread in his mouth – he was funny – and he came and he – gave me the other half-piece of sugar bread that he'd bought – and I ate it in one too – and he laughed and held out his hands and we – danced together. My brother Harold in his army uniform. Me in the red dress. And I – couldn't have been more happy. Silly, isn't it?

TWO. I think it's beautiful. May we try and make that memory for you?

BEATRICE *frowns*.

BEATRICE. That? You could do that?

TWO. If you want us to.

BEATRICE *thinks and her grief emerges brutally*.

BEATRICE. I lost him...

FOUR. In the war?

BEATRICE. No, love, four years back. Pneumonia. We were still in the same house, could you believe that? Neither of us married, it was always just the two of us. I nursed him, of course. As he went. And without him... But yes, dancing at the Fairbrass, that'll do.

She fades and is gone.

FIVE. Perry Como bliss. Delicious. Absolutely delicious. Wonderful work.

TWO. Can you confirm she was a suicide?

FIVE *checks through his paperwork. He frowns, surprised.*

FIVE. Where – did you get that from?

TWO. Am I right?

FIVE. Sometimes I think you're too good at this.

TWO *thinks and then nods.*

TWO. We'll send her off with something good.

FIVE. Next.

Scene Five

FOUR *is waiting in the hallway as* JILL *walks past.*

FOUR. Hi.

JILL. Oh. Hi.

FOUR. Sorry. Did I scare you?

JILL. No. I just – I thought we weren't allowed to talk outside our sessions with you – because –

FOUR. We can talk whenever you like. Loads of people stalk us actually, wanting to unload memory after memory. It can get a bit much.

JILL. Okay.

FOUR. Where are you going?

JILL. The toilets. Oh, the glamour...

   JILL *hesitates and then looks to move on.*

FOUR. Disneyland Paris, hey?

JILL. Yes. Have you been?

FOUR. No.

   Beat.

   But I feel like I have.

JILL. Oh, really.

FOUR. I mean, no offence, but we must have had thirteen teenage girls come through here and choose it.

JILL. What?

FOUR. Yeah. I don't know why. I mean, must be thirteen, yeah. And you're actually thirteen so that's neat, I guess.

JILL. Thirteen girls?

FOUR. Or fourteen, maybe fifteen, maybe twenty, you sort of lose count after a while.

JILL. Okay.

   She thinks. She makes a confused exit.

   Okay.

Scene Six

TWO *is watching some videotapes on a television on a trolley.*
FOUR *leans in.*

FOUR. Cat woman?

TWO. No.

FOUR. Then I'll stay. Don't like watching suicidal ones. Their
tapes are always so whahaha depressing.

*She walks in front of the television and starts looking
through the numbered tapes.*

I was thinking I could lead the next session maybe. Find a
way to –

TWO. If you want to make a complaint about the opportunities
you're getting, take it to Five. I'm working.

FOUR. Ouch.

*TWO looks at FOUR, unsure if he needs to say anything
else. He shakes his head and turns back to the tapes. There's
a pause.*

Who is it?

TWO. Mochizuki.

FOUR. Boring guy.

TWO. Yes. Boring guy.

He watches closely.

There's something about him I just can't figure out.

FOUR. Is that a committee meeting?

TWO. Please stop talking…

FOUR. He's not even saying anything…

TWO. It's not always about what they say but what they don't.

FOUR. What are they discussing?

TWO. Planning law.

FOUR *laughs*. TWO *looks up, a tiny bit amused*.

FOUR. Changed my mind, can we watch suicide lady's tapes please?

TWO (*laughing*). Changed my mind, can you get out please?

FOUR *ejects the tape and puts in another.*

FOUR. Live a little.

TWO. I have a system for this and –

FOUR. Your system just – brrrrroke.

FOUR *smiles. She exits.*

TWO *moves to change the tapes back, and then he stops. He stares at the screen.*

He's astonished.

KATIE. Take your blue shirt.

HIROKAZU. I've already packed my shirts.

KATIE. Take me to a restaurant, somewhere nice, and wear your blue shirt.

TWO *moves with urgency, and rewinds the tape.*

And the tape becomes somehow larger, it envelops the space.

HIROKAZU *and his wife* KATIE MOCHIZUKI *are packing for a holiday.*

We watch them engage in their activities.

Swimming costume? Might I need a swimming costume?

HIROKAZU. *Iranaiyo*. [Don't need it.]

KATIE. *Iranaino?* So we're not going to somewhere with a pool – or near the sea?

HIROKAZU. Stop digging.

KATIE. *Happy nanoyo*. [I'm happy.]

HIROKAZU. Don't be happy until we get there.

KATIE *looks at him and smiles.*

KATIE. Take your blue shirt.

HIROKAZU. I've already packed my shirts.

KATIE. Take me to a restaurant, somewhere nice, and wear your blue shirt.

HIROKAZU *smiles and bobs his head.*

And then TWO *walks up and is amongst them both, watching him and her.*

He pulls time backwards, he rewinds it.

Take your blue shirt.

Happy nanoyo.

HIROKAZU. Don't be happy until we get there.

KATIE. Take your blue shirt.

HIROKAZU. I've already packed my shirts.

He walks up close to KATIE. *He watches her imperceptibly small movements and a larger movement too, he doesn't want to miss a thing.*

KATIE. Take me to a restaurant, somewhere nice, and wear your blue shirt.

He rewinds the tape again.

Take your blue shirt. Take me to a restaurant, somewhere nice, and wear your blue shirt.

He rewinds the tape again.

Take me to a restaurant, somewhere nice, and wear your blue shirt.

And then KATIE *and* HIROKAZU *disappear and all that's left is* TWO.

Repeating every action carefully, almost like a dance, but not quite.

It's quite beautiful.

And then the music rises as the words are repeated. And others join TWO, *guides and guided…*

We travel into a sort of never-world.

The stage seems to open out again.

And our dead are walking through it.

Doing mundane tasks. Washing, eating, thinking, picking.

BEATRICE *is collecting leaves from the floor. She looks up at the sky. A projection screen behind her flashes images of her cat.*

JILL *walks past and suddenly we're thundering down the Tower of Terror.*

OBAFEMI *comes past and the image is replaced by a woman crying by a bed. She gets on her knees and she begins to pray.*

The audio tracks become layered over each other. Certain words stand out, others are lost to an ether of noise.

GEORGIE HANOY. 'Well, if we're going to get wet, we might as well be in our swimmers.' Which, I mean, the logic is there. But two weeks, camping, in Cornwall, just wearing swimming costumes, I mean it pushed me past the point of sanity. But it's all the insane memories I seem to hold on to. So can I have that? Me shivering in a tent with the kids, him swearing away trying to get the Calor gas stove lit for our supper, all of us laughing our arses off?

PRECIOUS MAPFUMO. My car with my children – and I look around and I look at them – and I know – I know – that life will never be better – and I'm filled with such unbelievable happiness.

OTTO BRADBURY. My son and I – on the stony beach – he'd just learnt to crawl backwards down the stairs – and this beach – it had these really steep banks – and I watched him – this intrepid little boy – pushing himself down the slope towards the sea, a bright smile on his face as if he was discovering something totally new.

And then the music stops. And TWO *stops. Standing alone.*

And then there's darkness. And there's someone standing in that darkness, GRAHAM JENKINS.

And TWO *is gone, and* FIVE *is now listening to him.*

GRAHAM JENKINS. It was weird but she had a bell on her bag and when she moved it'd go 'ding-a-ling'. So even if I were in another room, I knew she was coming as soon as I heard that bell. I quite… I really liked the sound of it. Well, more than liked. Then, when was it… Around winter… They don't like shoes in the house, so I was in the hall and putting on my shoes. It was night and pitch black… Anyway, I heard it, the ding-a-ling and even though I couldn't afford her that night, and even though I was just in my socks, I knew I had to follow her.

FIVE. Okay. And did you manage to catch her?

GRAHAM JENKINS. Oh yes.

FIVE. And – may I ask – what did you do to her when you caught up with her?

There's silence.

GRAHAM JENKINS. Oh yes.

And glimmering out of the darkness, as GRAHAM JENKINS *descends into it, are the words, written in neon letters on the filing cabinets, 'WEDNESDAY'.*

Scene Seven

A light rises on BEATRICE.

BEATRICE *carefully lays out a selection of goods on the table.*
TWO *watches her.*

TWO. Good morning. How are you, Miss Killick?

Pause. She stays intent on her task.

Apologies. You are busy.

BEATRICE. I've been collecting things.

TWO. I can see. That is good. I have things to show you too.
We have also got some fabric swatches for you to see – for
the red dress...

FOUR *puts down a book of swatches.*

BEATRICE. What red dress?

TWO. Fairbrass Hall. We think we've may have –

BEATRICE. Fairbrass? That place was knocked down years
ago, love. Derelict. Dirty. Infested. Drugs, you know. There
was a problem with bats. Drug people and bats.

TWO. We have been working on your memory.

BEATRICE. I know what I want for that, that's why I've
collected these pieces. My mother's cupboard, when I was a
little girl, I'd hide in there while my brother looked for me.
He wasn't good at it, or he was deliberately bad, and I'd sit in
there and it'd always smell of boots, you see, because it had
the outside boots. Perfectly dark with just the smell of boots.

TWO. You want the dark? You want your memory to be the dark?

BEATRICE. I am worried about my cat.

TWO. Miss Killick. Trust me when I tell you –

BEATRICE. Why should I trust you? When did you earn my
trust, pet?

TWO. We are here to help guide you –

BEATRICE. I want the dark. The smell of boots in the dark. The promise that he'll find me.

TWO. Please. Reconsider. Fairbrass Hall, your brother buying you the red dress –

BEATRICE. And see him? See him with his yellow face? Desperate. All the muscle wasted away.

TWO. That is not the memory of him you're taking –

BEATRICE. No one to help him but me. Calling for me. Telling me how much pain he was in? Unable to take any of it away. Unable to help the only man I ever loved. I want the dark. Give me the dark.

A buzzer sounds. The lights rise on the other side of the stage, where THREE *is talking to* HENRY.

FIVE. Number 427.

A buzzer.

Number 677.

THREE. What did you like as a child? Say the first thing that comes into your head.

HENRY. Planes.

THREE. Wonderful. Was there a trip you took – or did you just like to visit the airport?

HENRY. I was seven – maybe. It was during the divorce but before we – lost her. I had a model plane, a Cessna, that hung from my light on the ceiling – my grampy was a mechanic and built it for me himself. Anyway, I'd stand on my bed and close my eyes and I'd be sailing through the clouds. Butterflies all around me.

THREE. Butterflies?

HENRY. Green. Gold and... purple butterflies.

A buzzer sounds.

FIVE. Number 364.

A buzzer.

Number 271.

A buzzer.

Number 748.

The lights rise on the other side of the stage, where ONE *is talking to* OBAFEMI.

OBAFEMI. Explain it again – really slowly –

ONE. You have to choose a memory, you live in that memory –

OBAFEMI. No. I know that. Explain what you do. I want to understand you.

ONE. There's nothing to understand.

OBAFEMI. What did you do before this?

ONE. Please. Let me help you.

OBAFEMI. What's your name at least?

ONE *says nothing.*

I'll call you Sharon. There was a woman went to church with us called Sharon. Wouldn't ever sing. Stank of alcohol. Mum used to make me pray for her. But then Mum used to make me pray for everyone.

Beat. ONE *still says nothing.*

Why would you want to help me? You're not an angel. You're ordinary. Why would an ordinary woman want to help me?

ONE. You say ordinary with such disdain.

OBAFEMI. Is that wrong?

Beat.

What happens if I don't choose a memory?

ONE. You have to choose one. You have to. Trust me.

A buzzer sounds. JILL *is standing nervously.*

FIVE. Number 932.

A buzzer.

Number 114.

JILL. I think I was about three. It was the summer. I was resting my head on my mum's lap underneath the cherry-blossom tree. I remember how Mum smelled, how her scarf kept dripping down, its edges tickling me, how the blossom fell, and how my cheek felt, pressed against her lap. It was – comforting.

TWO. And that is what you'd like – you've changed your mind about the theme park?

JILL *looks at* FOUR.

JILL. Yes. Yes.

TWO. Then we will do our best to make cherry blossom work.

TWO *nods. He spots the look to* FOUR.

JILL. You think it's a good memory?

TWO. If it is the memory you want then it is a good memory.

JILL *nods and leaves. There's a silence.*

Had you talked to her?

FOUR. No.

TWO. You're lying.

FOUR. No.

TWO. You understand this is a delicate process.

FOUR. You're just in a shit mood because your old lady doesn't like you any more.

TWO. I don't think you're up to this job.

FOUR. Fuck you. I don't think I asked to do it.

TWO. That's enough! I will not have you cursing...

HIROKAZU. I'm sorry. You're busy.

HIROKAZU *is standing looking in at them both.*

FOUR. Mr Mochizuki, it's past dinnertime, you should be in your room –

TWO. Not so busy, come in.

HIROKAZU. Only if you're sure.

TWO. I apologise if you overheard our previous conversation. We are passionate about our jobs and –

HIROKAZU. I've been watching your tapes.

TWO. They are your tapes.

HIROKAZU. They don't feel like mine.

TWO. As I said to you at the beginning, they are just a reference point. They are the absolute truth, but we are not interested in the absolute truth, we are interested in memory.

HIROKAZU *looks at him carefully.*

HIROKAZU. Until I came here, I had a certain confidence about my life. But now... A so-so education, a so-so career, and a so-so marriage –

TWO. You told me it was a good marriage.

HIROKAZU. It was better than I deserved. It may sound strange to you, but we weren't brought together by burning passion.

TWO. That's not unusual. If anything it was normal for our generation.

Everything stops for a moment. TWO *winces.*

HIROKAZU. Did you just say 'our' generation?

TWO *hesitates. He looks up at* HIROKAZU. *And then he looks at* FOUR, *who takes a step back.*

TWO. Sorry, I was – sorry, I have been distracted and –

Beat.

HIROKAZU. You were – alive – once?

TWO. Yes.

HIROKAZU. The same time as me –

TWO. I was born on the 8th September 1941.

HIROKAZU. And you died – young?

TWO. I died as you find me.

HIROKAZU. I'm so sorry.

TWO. It was a long time ago.

> *Beat.* FOUR *steps back, visibly shocked by this new information.*

HIROKAZU. Did we know each other…?

TWO. There are systems in place to make sure that the guides and the guided are not – known – to each other.

HIROKAZU. The 'guides and the guided', I like that.

> *Beat.*

TWO. Have you chosen a moment for us, Mr Mochizuki?

HIROKAZU. I can't find my way through them – the tapes – they – uh – confuse me – I know I don't have long –

TWO. One more day. We can still do it. But you should sleep now.

> *He rises. He extends a hand.*

HIROKAZU. Thank you for taking so much care over me. I appreciate it.

> *He makes for the exit.*

TWO. No life is average.

HIROKAZU. One would hope not.

> *He exits.*

> *There's a silence.*

> FOUR *says nothing. She looks at* TWO, *who begins to tidy the room.*

FOUR. You're – seventy-nine?

TWO. Your maths is better than I presumed it might be.

FOUR. I had no idea –

TWO. Damn. That was a mistake.

Scene Eight

FIVE *is talking over a tannoy system.*

He is playing the accordian.

FIVE. A point of order. All those that have not settled on their
memory, you have twelve hours left to do so. Guides are
ready to see you whenever you'd need see us. Just submit a
blue form and you will be found.

He plays some other notes.

I've only been learning this five years. You wouldn't guess,
would you?

He smiles. He checks his notes.

Residents are reminded that bedrooms are for leisure time
not pleasure time. This remark is particularly directed
towards the Canadian contingent. As my father, who was in
the Merchant Navy, always told me – what's fine in Canada
is rarely fine anywhere else. Almost makes you want to visit,
doesn't it?

He plays the accordian again.

And now, to play you out, here's some good old George
Gershwin.

*He plays some George Gershwin, 'Someone to Watch Over
Me'. Badly.*

Wrong note. Wrong note. Wrong note.

Scene Nine

ONE, TWO *and* FOUR *sit out on the front of the stage, looking up at the stars.*

ONE. A black void.

TWO. Yes.

ONE. In which she can see nothing…

FOUR. Nothing at all. Apart from the smell of muddy boots. I don't understand. Fairbrass Hall…

ONE. Sometimes any memory at all hurts.

FOUR. But she could take something good…

TWO. I increasingly think these memories are not about happiest or best – meaningful or precious – it's most representative. It's the moment when your life felt most –

ONE. Like your life.

TWO. But what do I know?

ONE. Everything. (*To* FOUR.) You are aware he knows everything? Even Five goes to him for help.

TWO. I told someone when I died today.

ONE. Oh.

FOUR. He did as well. Full-moon week, maybe it does difficult things to us. Twists our desperate heads and –

TWO. It's always a full moon here.

FOUR. Is it? I hadn't – noticed.

> *Beat. She howls like a wolf. Then she laughs. But* TWO *is looking at her with a frown on his face.*

TWO. What difficult things has it done to you… the moon…

FOUR. Are the stars fake too?

ONE. The stars are pretty much fake in the other world too. Reflections of what was. Giant celestial farts.

TWO. You did? Didn't you? You talked to that poor girl. Got her to change her Disneyland Paris story.

FOUR. Accuse me one more time and I'll –

TWO. Our job is to guide, not influence –

FOUR. Weren't you trying to persuade the old lady? Wasn't that what you were doing? You're a fucking hypocrite.

TWO. This matters, you understand that? It's not a game, it matters.

FOUR. I know it's not a game. I know. I know.

TWO. I think you're still a teenage girl.

FOUR. Yes. I still am. A teenager in a teenage body trying to make sense of this place. What are you, Father Time?

ONE. Enough, okay? Both of you.

FOUR *walks away, full of anger.*

Oh, don't do that, I hate people who walk away in arguments, come on now...

FOUR *comes back.*

FOUR. You're supposed to be training me, you're supposed to be making me good enough to do this fucking job.

FOUR *looks at* TWO *a moment more and then walks hard away.*

ONE. Okay.

TWO. Say nothing.

ONE. What do you expect me to say?

TWO. Lots.

ONE. Well, imagine me saying it, okay? Imagine me saying it and you saying the right things back, about what you'll do in response.

He looks at her.

ONE. Why would you tell someone when you died?

TWO. It was a mistake.

ONE. You don't make mistakes.

TWO. It turns out I do.

ONE. Something is happening to you.

KATIE *appears,* TWO *sees her. And then pulls his eyes away.*

TWO. I'm fine. I am. We were going to talk about you. Let's talk about you.

ONE. Yeah.

Beat.

I don't stink of booze, do I?

KATIE *appears again.*

TWO. What?

ONE. Sorry. Ignore me. Being a silly arse.

TWO *can't take his eyes off* KATIE. ONE *notices.*

Oh, you are ignoring me, that's kind.

TWO. No. I was – listening – of course you don't stink of – why would you say that?

ONE. What's going on?

TWO. I can't say.

ONE. You can't or you won't?

TWO *looks at her.*

Be careful.

Scene Ten

BEATRICE *is collecting leaves and bits of twig, she puts them in her bag.* THREE *watches her.* BEATRICE *turns and looks at* THREE.

BEATRICE. Ah, you're one of the –

THREE. Yes.

BEATRICE. Are you hiding – have I spoilt your moment of hiding?

THREE. I don't think I have anything to hide from.

BEATRICE. Question: Is it always autumn here?

THREE. And a sunny day. I don't know why. Beyond my pay grade to know. I have news of your cat.

BEATRICE. You do?

THREE. Your cat is safe.

BEATRICE *looks suspicious.*

BEATRICE. What does she look like?

THREE. She's a tabby.

BEATRICE. She's not.

THREE (*sprung*). Worth a guess.

BEATRICE *turns back to her collecting. Desperately upset.*

Can I give you some advice?

BEATRICE. I loved that cat, you understand that? Lying about that, of all things…

THREE. The memory you take, it can free you or imprison you.

BEATRICE. Maybe I don't want –

She struggles for the word.

– freedom.

THREE. I understand you're angry.

BEATRICE. Everyone is angry! Didn't you notice? We wanted peace. Not this. Not this. Not choice. Peace. The choices to be over – over.

She starts to cry. THREE *gives her a handkerchief.*

THREE. If you want peace, look for it. It's there. If you're lucky.

He exits. BEATRICE *stands, swaying.*

FOUR *walks down the corridors.* JILL *runs after her.*

JILL. Excuse me. Excuse me.

FOUR. What?

JILL. Oh, you're upset, this is a bad time.

FOUR. No. I'm not upset. I'm not allowed to be upset. It's not my job. It's not the way I've been trained.

FOUR *is spitting with anger.* JILL *takes a step back, working her out.*

JILL. What? I don't understand.

FOUR. I'm busy. What do you want?

JILL. I wanted to – thank you.

FOUR *looks at her imperiously.*

FOUR. Well – it's better than Disneyland, right?

JILL. Yeah. Definitely. I mean, definitely.

FOUR. Mega. Well, see you.

JILL. 'Mega'? What kind of word is 'mega'?

FOUR. Is it… Do people not say that any more?

JILL. Did people ever say it?

FOUR *looks at* JILL, *studying her.*

Sorry. Sorry. It's a – good word.

FOUR. You really remember it? How your mother's lap felt and how she smelt?

JILL. And the cherry blossom, they will do the cherry blossom, right?

FOUR. You don't – remember, do you?

Beat.

JILL. Vaguely. Is that okay?

FOUR. It's your memory.

JILL. So you think I've made a mistake again?

FOUR. I think it's not my decision.

JILL *thinks and then nods and makes to walk away.*

I remember my dad's back when he carried me. It was broad and firm. And the smell of his sweat and how the gel in his hair stank.

JILL. My dad didn't wear hair gel.

FOUR. Yeah, well...

FOUR *hesitates a moment more. And then she nods and walks away.*

BEATRICE. So...

FOUR. Miss Killick? Is that you? What are you doing in the dark?

BEATRICE. What happens now? Now we've chosen a memory?

FOUR. We make them. Of course.

ACT TWO

Scene One

And suddenly there is blossom spilling from the ceiling.

TWO *stands underneath it. He's looking up.*

TWO. Too much? Get something to collect these petals. This could take some time.

FOUR (*offstage*). It looked okay.

TWO *talks into a walkie-talkie.*

Can we try it with less?

The tree keeps spilling blossom.

Less.

The tree spills a lot less blossom.

And now you've taken it too far.

He listens.

Somewhere between the two.

He listens.

Instinct.

He listens.

Yes. Instinct.

He listens.

No, I know that's not exactly scientific, but it's not science, is it?

He listens.

I'm aware you've studied it, and I have no doubt you know more about falling petals than I do. And yet –

He listens.

No, I'm not. I'm not. It's my client and it's a memory. Try somewhere between the two.

The tree spills a medium amount of blossom.

TWO *looks up with a frown.*

FOUR. Better?

TWO *thinks.*

Looks better to me.

TWO *gets on his knees.*

He looks out and then up. He holds his hand out. He smiles.

TWO. Yes, that feels right.

FOUR *kneels beside him.*

She looks up. She looks at TWO.

Yes?

FOUR. Yes.

She shuts her eyes.

Yes.

ONE *stands up from within the blossom. She's wearing a top hat with the word 'THURSDAY' imprinted on it in blossom.*

ONE. I like it.

TWO. But you're sentimental.

ONE. Sentimental isn't a bad thing in our job.

TWO. Do you think it'll take her back? She has no memory and I so want...

And amidst the blossom, FIVE *and* THREE *are revealed.*

FIVE. It's good. Thorough. Good. It'll take her back.

THREE. Where did we source the blossom? It's lifelike.

FOUR. It's paper.

THREE. No!

FOUR. Three little ladies cut them for us.

TWO. Little ladies?

FOUR. I can say that. I am a little lady. Three Little Ladies from Northampton.

THREE. From Northampton. Even better.

He looks around the faces.

FIVE. I'll say what I say every week: This is always the moment when our job feels like the greatest honour.

THREE. And I'll add what I always add: The greatest honour and the greatest burden.

FIVE. Is everyone ready?

ONE. We're ready.

FIVE. Then let's begin.

Scene Two

TWO *is showing* BEATRICE *around the set*. FOUR *trails behind them*.

TWO. We're – every decision is about accentuating the red – as you can see –

BEATRICE. I don't quite…

TWO. It's a trick of the eye. If you keep the background monochrome – it heightens the impact.

BEATRICE. Oh, yes, I think I… see…

TWO. We have been working on the best sugar-bread recipe. How much sugar to how much bread.

BEATRICE. Oh, that seems – unnecessary –

TWO. Try it.

> FOUR *proffers a tray of sugar bread. Both* TWO *and* BEATRICE *take a piece.*

BEATRICE. It's – um – good.

TWO. We can probably do better. You deserve the best.

> *He looks offstage, he nods.*

> And here is the bit I've been most looking forward to – Beatrice, I'd like you to meet Harold...

> *A young straight-backed man walks forward. He's in partial army uniform. This is* ACTOR HAROLD.

> BEATRICE *takes a moment, swaying on the spot. Slightly – no, scrub that – entirely overwhelmed by the face in front of her.*

BEATRICE. He's too –

> *She struggles for the word.*

> – young, isn't he?

TWO. No.

BEATRICE. He looks – just like him.

TWO. Thank you. He's French, in fact, but – as we see it – there's no need for dialogue.

> *A record player is wound up by* ACTOR HAROLD.

> BEATRICE *looks around herself, this is too much.*

> And this is – you...

> *A young woman in a partially made dress walks towards them – this is* ACTRESS BEATRICE. *The real* BEATRICE *gasps.*

> She's wearing something very provisional – what we call a toile – It's not quite right yet, I'm just waiting for some colour samples, then we'll start again. But she does have –

BEATRICE. I almost can't look at her.

TWO nods, 'The Red Shoes' begins to play on the record player.

TWO. The one thing we've struggled with is deciding on the definitive steps for 'The Red Shoes. So we did wonder if –

BEATRICE. I've forgotten them.

TWO. You probably haven't, if you try.

BEATRICE looks at the girl.

BEATRICE. It's quite extraordinary.

TWO. You lead.

BEATRICE takes a step towards the girl. The girl takes BEATRICE's arms. Ready to be instructed.

BEATRICE. Is she English?

TWO. Polish.

BEATRICE. Wonderful.

She looks into the girl's eyes.

Hello.

They start to gently dance.

Scene Three

FIVE *is sitting in a dormitory room.*

FIVE. I'm here to help you.

OBAFEMI. You're the guy who runs the place, right? The tannoy guy.

FIVE. Correct. I am the 'tannoy guy'. And my colleague has asked me to come to talk to you –

OBAFEMI. That's nice – of your colleague.

FIVE. She is concerned –

OBAFEMI. She's right to be.

FIVE. Concerned that you won't be able to find a path out of here.

OBAFEMI. What happens if we don't? She won't say.

FIVE. There is not an option.

OBAFEMI. I'm guessing it's nothing. I'm guessing it's just a void. An eternal… Well, I'll take it.

FIVE *loses it.*

FIVE. Jesus Christ!

OBAFEMI. What?

FIVE. She said you were a wanker, but even I am surprised at how much of a wanker you actually are.

There's a shocked silence.

OBAFEMI. Are you allowed to say that?

FIVE. Oh yes.

OBAFEMI *looks at him. Finally someone to fight fire with.*

OBAFEMI. You don't know my story.

FIVE. I know enough.

OBAFEMI. You're fucking rude.

FIVE. Thanks for fucking noticing.

OBAFEMI. You been here the longest? Of everyone? You look the oldest?

FIVE. How gracious of you to say. I've been here for long enough, let's say that.

OBAFEMI. What's the worst thing you've been asked to recreate? A rape? A murder? The abuse of a child?

FIVE. I haven't ever been asked to recreate any of those things –

OBAFEMI. But you do get these men and women come through here.

FIVE. Fine. You want a sensible answer. You can have one. I consider my job to be like that of a surgeon. Not to sit in judgement, rather to do my best for everyone who lies on my table.

OBAFEMI. You're not a surgeon, cowboy.

FIVE. But neither am I a cowboy. I'm bloody good at my job if you'll give me the chance.

OBAFEMI. I should have been judged! They said I'd be judged!

FIVE. Good, finally some truth. It's nonsense but I can see you feel it.

OBAFEMI. Why is it 'nonsense'?

FIVE. Because you've misunderstood this place and fundamentally misunderstood judgement.

Beat. This sinks deep.

FIVE *considers and then plunges on.*

I had a murderer once. It wasn't clear initially, then it became very clear. He'd killed many women. He asked for a memory of swimming naked in the sea with his father. They didn't speak, just swam. He must have been nine years old in it. I didn't question what it meant. Perhaps he thought he could be eventually washed clean. Perhaps it was a memory that was free of his hatred. Perhaps it was the source of his hatred. Personally, I think that's why we recreate memories rather than replicating moments, you can't quite wash the life off a created memory. It's stained, you see, with what you became. I believe he took his murders with him, just as you would take your sorrow. And that's why I say there is judgement, so much judgement, in what we do here. But it is not the judgement you were expecting. It is your own judgement, of the man you are. And perhaps our own judgement is the only judgement that truly counts. Perhaps our own judgement is always the most damning.

Beat.

If you don't cross you become one of us, that's what happens.

OBAFEMI. And that's bad, is it?

FIVE. Depends how you feel about those that can't be judged.

OBAFEMI *takes this in.*

OBAFEMI. I can't forgive it.

FIVE. What?

OBAFEMI. This place. Existing. I can't forgive it.

FIVE *thinks and then nods.*

FIVE. Ah, kid. Most days I can't forgive it either.

He throws him a packet of Maltesers and exits.

OBAFEMI. Maltesers? Where the hell did you get Maltesers from? Answer me. Come on… Answer me.

FIVE. Look for answers and you won't find them, enjoy questions and you'll have a really nice life. Now there's a motto I can't live by.

Scene Four

TWO *walks past a man sorting through pebbles for a beach, a cloud manufacturer, and someone dragging a large aeroplane propeller.*

He sees HIROKAZU *waiting for him.*

TWO. Mr Mochizuki.

HIROKAZU. Please. Call me Hirokazu – Hiro.

TWO *nods. There's a silence.*

I still haven't an answer for you. I haven't a memory. I'm sorry.

TWO. We can stretch to another day. It gives us less time to prepare but we can do amazing things in twenty-four hours.

HIROKAZU looks at TWO, working him out.

HIROKAZU. Why do you care about me? The tapes, the constant cajoling –

TWO. It's my job to care.

Beat. TWO thinks and then sits beside HIROKAZU.

HIROKAZU. No. There's something else. We did, didn't we? We knew each other. I can – feel it somehow.

TWO looks up, sprung.

TWO. No.

Beat.

But – I did – I knew your wife.

HIROKAZU looks at him carefully.

HIROKAZU. How?

TWO. That's more difficult. Katie and I… I – before you met her I'm certain of that – she and I – I'm sorry I – loved her.

And now the truth is here.

HIROKAZU. And she loved you.

The information just sits between them. Like a polished stone.

She even showed me your photograph once. I see it so clearly now – I should have – I see it so clearly.

He thumps his leg.

Mattaku ahoda!

TWO. Please accept my sincerest apologies. I will find you a new guide. I will get you the time you need and you will not see me again.

HIROKAZU. No. I want you. To stay. As my guide.

There's a silence.

TWO. Our relationship is compromised at best, ugly at worst –

HIROKAZU. You offer me eternity. She is all I want to spend eternity with – you're a decent man, and well – you loved her too, with your help maybe I can understand how to.

TWO. You had the life I wanted. I can't help you.

HIROKAZU *roars back.*

HIROKAZU. *AND YOU WERE THE MAN I WANTED TO BE, SO YOU HAVE TO.*

There's a silence. A tear drips from HIROKAZU*'s eye, he wipes it away, irritated.*

TWO. I requested her tapes.

HIROKAZU. She has tapes too? Of course she does.

TWO. I requested them – for me. Which breaks – every rule there is. I am not a decent man. I am not who you need here.

There's a silence.

HIROKAZU *rubs another angry tear from his eye.*

HIROKAZU. You remember the strange way she'd insist on eating biscuits? The way she'd eat cereal with water on top.

TWO. And insist it tasted better? Sure.

HIROKAZU. Her ability to empty her mind just before going to sleep – spilling out every worry she has –

TWO. Have we enough money for the rent?

HIROKAZU. Have we enough for the mortgage? And then turning over and sleeping soundly whilst you lie awake thinking –

TWO. Well, have we?

HIROKAZU. The rash she'd get every time she ate clams?

TWO (*at the same time*). Clams. And her insistence on eating them all the same.

HIROKAZU. The way she'd judge people within three minutes of meeting them –

TWO. And you'd know exactly what she thought. Whether you liked it or not.

HIROKAZU *smiles*.

HIROKAZU. I'm lost. I need someone who knows her. You do.

TWO *thinks a thousand thoughts*.

TWO. Maybe we should – could – watch them – the tapes – together.

HIROKAZU. I would like that.

Scene Five

And suddenly the stage is alive with movement, everyone getting the final pieces of the jigsaw ready. We hop between them as they argue their way to solution. A fold-up ladder is brought across the stage with 'FRIDAY' sculpted between its rungs.

Our numbers talk to stage management via walkie-talkie.

FOUR. We're waiting for delivery on half a dozen rocks – can you make sure they get here –

ONE. You sent me an actor but they weren't appropriate. They wouldn't shave their beard… Of course they do, I needed a nineteenth-century Russian soldier, they didn't allow beards in the Russian army –

THREE. I've had just about enough of this. Did I not explain to you? YOU ARE SLOPPY. DO YOU HEAR ME? SLOPPY AND POOR. WILL YOU LISTEN TO ME – LISTEN TO ME –

FIVE *cuts* THREE*'s walkie-talkie cable*.

Hello?… Hello?

FIVE. Please don't worry. I'll be listening to him so you don't
have to. Thank you for all you do, and all you try to do.
You're appreciated.

He disconnects. THREE *is glowering.* FIVE *signals for* ONE
to leave. She does.

If you're going to hit me, aim for the ears not the chin. The
ears I have no pride about, the chin – it's rather a splendid
chin, don't you think?

THREE. They've sent me a Piper not a Cessna –

FIVE. Neither of these names mean anything to me.

THREE. A Cessna is a high-winged monoplane. A Piper is not.
If we can't recreate with exactitude then why are we here?

FIVE. I like it when you're commanding.

THREE. Imagine you're a seven-year-old boy. Look out as if
you're in a plane.

FIVE. I'm finding you very sexually attractive right now.

THREE. The wings are in front of you – what you see the world
through, how can we recreate what my client saw if the
wings are in the wrong place?

FIVE *looks up.*

FIVE. You know what I always say – the actual isn't interesting
– it's the feeling – what did he feel about that Cessna and
how might we recreate it? That's the magic.

THREE *looks at him, dourly.*

THREE. Were you a teacher? Before all this?

FIVE. Do I seem like a teacher?

THREE. You remind me of one.

But with that is acceptance that it'll do. THREE *makes to
exit.*

FIVE. You are very good at your job.

THREE. Geography. I bet you taught geography.

THREE *exits*. TWO *is lingering behind*. FIVE *frowns*.

FIVE. If I was still alive I'd siphon off his sweat, bottle it and sell it. I'd call it 'rage'. Would make me a fortune. And the whole world angry.

TWO. I've made a mistake.

FIVE *turns to look at him*.

FIVE. You haven't said something like that for quite some time.

TWO. I don't know that I am doing the right thing. In fact, I know I'm doing the wrong thing.

FIVE. I supervise only because you didn't want the job. You've been here far longer than I. I can't claim to captain you. You're the one I come to for advice.

TWO *looks at him*.

Go on.

TWO. I got given someone – who turned out to be the husband of the woman I – was with – before I – died.

FIVE. Oh.

TWO. He wants me to stay with him. I told him that's not going to happen. He keeps insisting. But he hasn't found a memory and I think that's probably my fault.

TWO *starts to cry*.

FIVE. Oh. Okay. Where's that from?

TWO *continues to cry*. FIVE *moves towards him*. TWO *raises a hand,* FIVE *stops*.

Like a frozen pipe, isn't it? When it thaws, it comes out dangerously fast.

TWO. I feel ashamed – but also – so excited. For so long she's been all I'd thought about. I looked at the moon and I'd see her face. I looked at this chair and she'd be in it. I looked at the wall and her body would be curled inside it – there in the cracks and the dirt and the… And now I can actually see her and –

Beat.

I've been in control for so long, you know, and then suddenly – suddenly – I'm not and I don't know whether to –

Beat.

Say something. Please.

KATIE *appears behind* TWO.

FIVE. You may have let him down. You may not. But don't ask me to judge you. I don't have it in me.

TWO *looks up.*

TWO. We watch together – we watch her birthday cake get accidentally left on the top of her dad's car – we watch her get christened. We watch her learn the clarinet.

FIVE. The devil's instrument.

KATIE *starts to walk forward.* TWO *and her start moving as one.*

TWO. We watch her get her first boyfriend which I thought was me but is actually a man called Simon.

FIVE. The devil's name.

TWO. And then I come along. And I look like a stranger. And we watch her with me. The time we went to London and missed our bus home and spent the night walking the streets together.

FIVE. The devil's city.

THREE *closes his eyes.*

KATIE. Charlie. Charlie. Keep up.

TWO. I'm trying to.

KATIE. You're not trying to – you can run faster than me. You want to miss the bus.

TWO. You're saying it's some kind of evil plan?

KATIE. My mother will kill you.

TWO. She may. But that's a problem for tomorrow and what a night we'll have.

A gentle irrepresible dance is formed between KATIE *and* TWO.

I kissed her in Green Park, Hyde Park and Victoria Park that night. It was the best of my life.

FIVE. It sounds rather excessive.

TWO. We hadn't ever – we didn't do anything that was disrespectful but even so – we got to watch the sun rise sitting beside the River Thames. It was magical.

FIVE. Sounds lovely. I'd have booked a cheap hotel and had my way. But, you know, each to their own.

TWO *laughs*.

TWO. We watch every intimacy of our relationship. Good and bad.

KATIE. Get away from me. Get away.

TWO. I saw how you were looking at him.

KATIE. How I was looking at who? I don't even know who you're bloody talking about.

TWO. I was jealous, a lot, and I'd forgotten.

FIVE. We all forget our truths.

Beat.

TWO. And then it happens – I die.

There's a silence.

She doesn't have tape of that. She wasn't there.

Beat.

Hiro mostly says nothing, though I find myself holding his hand as she cries by my grave. And then – from then on – of course – I'm not there, and then – he is. And I have to watch them. The puzzle of them. And it makes me want to rip out my eyes.

Beat.

FIVE. I will step in if you ask me to. It sounds like you're not being safe with him or yourself.

TWO looks at him.

But maybe you've been safe with yourself for too long. Frozen pipes shouldn't stay frozen.

Beat.

TWO. Why weren't you able to cross, Peter? I've never asked.

FIVE. No. You haven't.

Beat. He smiles.

And that – I think – is how it should stay.

Scene Six

TWO walks through a never-world of memory reconstruction. This is backstage at the greatest show on earth. Large feathers are transported across the stage, followed by a blackboard, followed by a street lamp.

TWO turns and looks around himself, and then ONE barrels past.

ONE. You seen an actor? Tall. Cambodian. He's late for his call.

THREE passes through in the other direction.

THREE. Don't talk to me. Don't talk to me. Someone's lost an aeroplane. How can you lose an aeroplane?

And then suddenly BEATRICE *is standing in front of* TWO. *She's walking very slowly, contemplating the sky.*

BEATRICE. I hadn't noticed it before. Your stars are entirely out of alignment.

TWO. Are they?

BEATRICE. Orion's Belt. Do you see? It looks more like Orion's Knickers. It's got a gusset to it. A cluster just there.

TWO. Oh. Yes. Is that right?

BEATRICE. I'm pleased I've found you.

TWO. I'm not letting you go back to the cupboard. I don't have time to make it.

BEATRICE. Buck up, young man.

TWO. Sorry?

BEATRICE. Buck up.

TWO. Have you had a personality transplant?

BEATRICE. No. I've found some – I've found a – I've found something worthwhile – and – uh – buck up.

TWO. You keep saying that and I have no idea what you mean.

BEATRICE. You're – moping. My brother used to mope. I was always telling him: Buck up.

TWO. There's a way you say it that is particularly intimidating.

BEATRICE. Thank you.

TWO *smiles.*

And thank you. I am – considerably looking forward to what you've made for me. I consider it quite a gift.

TWO. My pleasure.

BEATRICE. My gift in return is to tell you: Buck up.

She looks at him. He smiles.

TWO. I'll do my best.

Scene Seven

FOUR *enters wearing angel wings and a halo. She is listening to 'Heaven Must Be Missing an Angel' by Tavares on her Walkman and dancing along in her own world.* TWO *enters surreptitiously and then she notices and* FOUR *jumps a mile.*

FOUR. Jesus fucking Christ.

TWO. You are aware, we wear those for them – not us.

FOUR. Just – trying things out...

TWO. It suits you.

FOUR. It's not meant to suit me.

He smiles.

TWO. I once had a man so convinced I was an angel that he asked to put his fingers in my mouth. Apparently, I'm not sure why – he believed angels didn't have saliva – that's the tell – not wings – no saliva.

FOUR. Did you let him?

TWO. No.

FOUR. I'd have spat at him.

TWO. And that's why you deserve that outfit and I don't. Though if you get sweat marks in it, costume will kill you.

FOUR (*outraged*). 'Sweat marks!'

TWO *smiles again.*

TWO. I had a visit. From Jill Smart. She said you'd told her the truth, she said you had intimidated her –

FOUR. Is that it then? Am I out?

TWO. – but then you set it right. She said that she thought you were lovely. And then she backed out the room – shy and embarrassed.

FOUR *looks at him.*

It took me – when I arrived here – a long time to work out what to do – how to be – I wanted to fail – I wanted to see what would happen if I failed and then it just became easier to – try –

FOUR. Better? Or just easier?

He smiles at her – a great question.

TWO. Easier and better, though it took me even longer to see that.

Beat.

You did a good thing.

HIROKAZU. Charlie. CHARLIE.

FOUR. Who's Charlie?

TWO. Hiro? Are you okay?

HIROKAZU *runs across the stage.*

HIROKAZU. Charlie, I've been looking for you everywhere – I've found it, I've found a moment. I've found a moment. I've found a moment.

TWO *turns and looks at him.*

You helped. You truly did help.

HIROKAZU *focuses and refocuses.*

A bench. Just a bench. She has met me in her lunch break. We sit by the lake in the park, there are some Canadian geese visiting and we've been watching them nest. She's upset, a hard morning. There are things going on at work she doesn't like. I've made us both lunch and it's – awful. A pasta salad that Delia recommended and I absolutely mess up. The eighties you know – we thought pasta salad was very cutting edge. She reveals the secret sandwiches she brought just in case. We laugh. She's pleased to see me – talk to me – I lift her up and allow her to go on with her day. I don't feel she loves me in that moment – I do feel I am her best friend. The man she spent her life with. A good man. In her eyes at least.

HIROKAZU *looks at* TWO.

Can you make that memory for me? Even at this late hour?

FOUR. I'm afraid you're past cut–

TWO. It's just a bench. It would be our honour.

HIROKAZU *thanks him with a nod.*

HIROKAZU. You think it a good one?

TWO. I do.

HIROKAZU*'s eyes fill with tears.*

HIROKAZU. And do you think – do you think – it's one she'd have liked me to choose?

TWO. I think it's one she'd have loved you to choose.

HIROKAZU *smiles, and then nods.*

And then he comes back and he hugs TWO *tightly.*

The two men hold each other for what feels like an age.

And then HIROKAZU *makes his way slowly away.*

FOUR *looks at* TWO.

FOUR. That's your name? Charlie?

TWO. It was.

FOUR. How come he knew it and I don't?

TWO. He needed to.

FOUR. Do you know my name too?

TWO. Of course I do.

Beat.

FOUR. Charlie. You don't look like a Charlie.

Beat.

Seems like you did a good thing too.

There's a silence.

Are you crying? You're crying, aren't you? Oh no, you're an ugly cryer. Stop crying, it really doesn't suit you.

He hits her with a pillow.

She hits him back.

They have a pillow fight that ends with a shower of feathers descending and ascending across the stage.

Scene Eight

FIVE *is sitting at the controls.*

FIVE. It's that man again. It's late. You need to get to your beds. I'll be quick.

He drinks from a cup of tea.

That sound effect is supplied by me failing to drink a cup of tea properly. I don't apologise for it. I've a crooked tongue, if you couldn't tell, and crooked tongues always lead to slurping. You can't beat slurping down a good cup of tea if you've a crooked tongue like mine.

He looks down at his notes.

Some housekeeping. All those worrying about the blown fuses. Don't. People are simply making themselves look as good as they can and they're overloading the system. Don't complain. Don't pass judgement. They must do as they do, you must do as you do. We can all cope with the occasional blackout.

He smiles. He composes himself.

A final word. There is a phrase – my mother used to say – many a mickle makes a muckle. It means that a lot of small amounts, put together, make a large amount. It is an honour to be responsible for you all for this week, and I tell you – every single one of you has significance in the stars above.

He sits back.

By which I mean, yes, you're all mickles and yes, you'll find your place in the muckle.

He laughs.

Wherever you travel tomorrow, I hope you find a pleasant rest.

Beat.

And whoever stole my squeeze-box, please give it back.

Scene Nine

ONE *is facing* OBAFEMI.

ONE. Your final chance.

OBAFEMI. You think you could still make something for me now –

ONE. Give me the chance to.

OBAFEMI *smiles.*

OBAFEMI. No. I'm fine.

ONE. Aren't you scared?

OBAFEMI. Scared? That's a big word to use.

He looks at her.

I was scared of death. I was scared of dying. This – no.

ONE. I just think you should reconsider –

OBAFEMI. I first became ill when I was fourteen. I was starting to make sense of the world. There were girls interested in me. I was starting to become a man. And then suddenly I was just an ill person – just a victim.

ONE. There must have been happy times – precious and
meaningful times –

OBAFEMI. Of course there were. But I was always sick in them.

ONE. Okay.

OBAFEMI. I don't want to be trapped in the world of a
thirteen-year-old kid, who doesn't know what age feels like,
and I don't want to be trapped in an ill body.

ONE *says nothing*.

I know what happens now. Your boss told me. I know what
happens.

ONE. And still you choose it?

OBAFEMI. Yes, I choose this – I choose you – I choose
whatever this life is.

ONE. You'll watch the possibilities of other lives – you'll make
happiness for them – and you'll –

Beat.

They give us a day, you know, to reset, recharge, they give
us Sunday – and do you know what we do in it?

OBAFEMI. Go wild?

ONE. We sit in our rooms and avoid each other. For it is when
there's nothing to do that the pain truly comes.

She walks away. He stares after her.

Scene Ten

TWO, FOUR *and* FIVE *enter the space pushing a boat. On its
side is written the word 'SATURDAY'*.

*The scene opens with '(Looking for) The Heart of Saturday
Night' by Tom Waits.*

THREE *enters and looks at them. He checks his watch.*

And now – well, to describe it wouldn't do it justice, because I don't know what it looks like.

But, brilliantly, visions come to life.

Boats are captained, cars are driven, stony beaches are crawled down, dark dens are sat in, blossom trees drop blossom, tents are rained on, swimming costumes are worn, and BEATRICE *dances.*

Yes, BEATRICE KILLICK *dances. She dances with a wonder. An entirely physical beautiful sequence, that will remove breath from bodies and hair from heads.*

And of course a plane flies.

It will be beautiful, it will be extraordinary, it will be eternity people will want to live in.

And as their dreams are enacted so eternity takes them, people are lost to the ether forever.

And as they do so only their shoes are left. With smoke rising from them. The ash remains of all that was.

We save the best for the last – a young couple sitting on a bench.

They dance a beautiful dance.

And then HIROKAZU *is gone. Leaving his shoes like all the others did.*

And everything is gone.

The guides stand watching the space the memory show was in.

There's a silence. Which is half contentment at a job well done – and half jealousy.

Jealousy from everyone but TWO *– who has an extraordinary look on his face.*

TWO. He chose well. Don't you think?

ONE. He chose very well. A nice place to stay, I think.

FOUR. A nice place for a nice man.

THREE. A beautiful choice.

FIVE. An excellent week of work. Well done, everybody.

TWO looks at FIVE.

TWO. What if – the week isn't quite – over?

FOUR. What?

TWO. It is still Saturday, right? Is there time for one more?

There's a shocked silence. Even TWO is shocked he's saying this.

ONE. You want to pass?

TWO. I feel like this is what my life has been building to.

ONE. Your life ended a long time ago.

TWO. My life here. I was waiting for Hirokazu Mochizuki.

They all look at FIVE.

FOUR. No. He can't. We haven't prepared.

THREE. We haven't prepared at all.

FIVE. If you're feeling like you might be ready then let's discuss it through next week and –

TWO. I'd like it to be now.

FIVE. Whatever makes you think that –

TWO. I've finally done something good.

FIVE. We all do something good every day. We certainly do it every week –

TWO. Something that makes sense of me – of this – of why I'm here –

FIVE. We're not here for a reason, we're here for the absence of a reason.

TWO. Please. I've waited a long time for this moment. I don't want to wait any longer. Don't deny me this.

Beat. FIVE *and* TWO *hold eyes.*

THREE. Yes. He will.

FIVE. Charlie, I have to be certain this isn't some emotional impulse to –

TWO. Everything is an emotional impulse, Peter. This is what we're expected to do. Treat me like any other client. This – is what I want.

THREE *is looking at* FIVE, *he sees something he doesn't like.*

THREE. Don't you dare be swayed –

FIVE *is emotional, but powerful.*

FIVE. This is my centre. I decide the numbers. I decide what can happen. If he wants to go, he – goes.

Beat. TWO *wants to hug* FIVE *but doesn't.*

But we'll have to move faster than we ever have. Have you a memory you'd like to choose? For you and Katie? We can fetch the actress back. The two of you – beside a river as the sun rises.

TWO. No. That would feel disrespectful. To Hiro. And to her.

THREE. He doesn't even have a memory. I've heard of officers passing, but always with preparation –

TWO. I would like this.

They all turn to him.

FIVE. What?

TWO. I would like this. What we did here.

FIVE. This is not a memory from your life.

TWO. I would like to sit here and look out at all of you.

FOUR. Look at us?

ONE. Come on, you know that's not possible...

THREE. It has to be a memory from your living past.

TWO. This is my memory. And it's a happy one.

FIVE. It breaks every rule.

TWO. It's what I want. Will you let it happen? Please.

FIVE *thinks*.

FIVE. Just sitting here?

TWO. Just sitting.

FIVE. Just like that?

THREE. Are you serious?

TWO. Looking out at you all. The people that make the work happen. The work I know is tremendously hard. But the work I'm finally proud to have been a part of.

They all look at him, astonished.

ONE. You want to take us with you?

TWO *blinks back tears*.

TWO. Yes please. I do.

There's a long silence.

FIVE. Then let's take our positions.

THREE. No. No. He can't –

FIVE. Yes. He can. Because we make the impossible happen here, don't we?

FIVE *looks at* THREE *who – pained for a moment – accepts it with a nod. He sits. He looks up at* TWO. *Nothing need be said between them.*

ONE *and* FOUR *linger a moment more.*

ONE. This I wasn't expecting.

TWO. No.

There's a pause.

ONE. You're sure? You're absolutely sure?

TWO. For the first time in a long time.

ONE. And what does that feel like?

TWO. You'll find a way. You will.

Beat. ONE *walks away. Trying to process that.*

FOUR *is left.*

You're ready. You've learnt your last lesson.

FOUR. But...

TWO takes her in his arms and kisses her forehead.

TWO. You're ready, and so am I.

FOUR. Don't. Please. Leave us. Leave me.

TWO. But I'm not leaving you. I'm taking you with me. You're coming with me. You understand that?

FOUR. You know how I feel about you, right?

TWO. Rachel. You'll be fine.

FOUR. What if I can't do this without you?

He pauses a moment more.

TWO. You can. And if you get bored along the way – this is a mega good book.

He puts it down on the floor.

She laughs, thinks, and then nods, wipes her tears and takes her place.

FIVE. We say nothing?

TWO. All I need to do is look at you.

FIVE. Go – with our love...

ONE. The love we have.

FIVE. Go with all we have to give you.

THREE. And if all we have is envy?

FIVE. Then try to find beauty in envy. See the ambition in it.

FIVE *walks back to his seated position.*

Is this right?

TWO *nods. There's a silence. He smiles.*

TWO. Thank you.

TWO *sits on the chair.*

Music rises.

He bows his head.

He looks up. His eyes look at all his colleagues in turn.

And then he fades away.

Leaving just a pair of shoes behind.

Scene Eleven

And then the sign comes up:

'SUNDAY'.

And there's nothing.

And then it fades away.

ACT THREE

Scene One

ONE, THREE *and* FOUR *are cleaning up the room and sorting and boxing the shoes, as we saw in the opening sequence.* OBAFEMI *is making some limited effort to join in.*

FOUR. You've got to watch out for the sexy ones...

OBAFEMI. I'm not frightened of sexy.

FOUR. The ones who want to tell you about every sexual adventure they've ever had. It can get quite graphic.

OBAFEMI. I'll take my kicks where I get them.

FOUR *looks at him, outraged.*

FOUR. That's – you can't say that!

OBAFEMI. I don't mean everything I say.

FOUR *looks at him, trying to work him out.*

FOUR. You probably won't get it so bad – given how you're a guy –

OBAFEMI. I'm a guy, am I? Not a man, a guy.

FOUR. You are such a guy.

THREE. Don't listen to her, you'll be fine.

FOUR. He'll be more than fine, all the teenage girls are so going to fancy you.

ONE. She means she fancies you.

FOUR. That is outrageous. Take that back.

ONE. I take it back. But I still said it.

FOUR. I hate you.

ONE. You hate everyone.

OBAFEMI *stops, he looks around the room – slightly overwhelmed.*

OBAFEMI. How do we do it? How do we give them what they want?

ONE. We listen.

FOUR. We learn.

THREE. We help.

ONE *has twisted the chairs so that 'MONDAY' is spelt out of their backs and fronts.*

FIVE. Okay. Okay.

FIVE *enters at speed.*

Last week, we managed to send through twenty-two, including our colleague Charlie. Splendid work which I'm grateful for. Unfortunately, there was also one who wasn't able to pass. He will be remaining with us, working as an assistant for a while. Please give him your support.

ONE. He has it.

FIVE. Welcome.

OBAFEMI. Thank you.

FIVE. We've got nineteen coming through today. You'll take eight.

He hands eight to ONE.

And eight for you.

He hands eight to THREE.

Leaving three for you.

FOUR *is handed the files.*

FOUR. I won't let you down.

FIVE *smiles kindly.*

FIVE. I wish you all a good week.

He checks his watch.

ONE. Do we have clearance?

FIVE. Well. We haven't long.

Blackout.

And as the audience leave we play all the tapes we haven't yet, we play them in the foyer too and especially in the toilets. The chosen memories of many people. We leave them in their own contemplation.

Hopefully there is beauty there.

www.nickhernbooks.co.uk

facebook.com/nickhernbooks

twitter.com/nickhernbooks